Management Steps of Success (S.O.S.)

<u>4 BASIC POINTS</u>

Train, Motivate, Delegate, Follow Up

author
George Kaminsky

authorHOUSE™

1663 LIBERTY DRIVE, SUITE 200
BLOOMINGTON, INDIANA 47403
(800) 839-8640
WWW.AUTHORHOUSE.COM

First published by AuthorHouse 07/07/2005

ISBN: 1-4208-3596-3 (sc)

Printed in the United States of America
Bloomington, Indiana

This book is printed on acid-free paper.

MANAGEMENT

Steps of Success

(S.O.S.)

For the:

* Up and Coming Manager

* Recently Promoted Manager

* Most Experienced Manager

* New Business Owner

* Experienced Business Owner

PREFACE

It is time to move the textbooks and theories aside! This book is powerful and will take you on a journey through "real life" experiences of managing employees. It will cut to the chase and is formatted as a quick reference guide, with topics that are concise, to the point, and easy to read. Keep it in your office to refer to, as it will keep you inspired while you take on the difficult job of managing employees. There are five chapters, consisting of: The Manager, The Employee, Managing Employees, Goals and Expectations, and Achieving Results. The four basic points: TRAIN, MOTIVATE, DELEGATE, and FOLLOW UP are a constant reminder of effective leadership skills. This book is down to earth, using quotes and illustrations, and is written solely from twenty-plus years of management experience and training. You will not lose interest with its remarkable truth and humor!

TABLE of CONTENTS

INTRODUCTION

* Inspiration and Goals

* Competition—"Piece of the Pie"

* Why Do Companies Struggle to Be Profitable?

* Sick of Work—Gone Fishing!

* Increase Revenue/Reduce Expenses

* Manager "Report Card"

INSPIRATION AND GOALS
Of The Author

In writing this book, my mission is to inform and inspire other managers to be the best. This book is easy to read, humorous, and written to speak directly to the reader.

I was motivated to write management books after becoming aware of the quality of managers in the business world. I worked for too many managers that, in my opinion, lacked the "people skills" necessary to be effective. These individuals were intelligent when it came to budgets and decision making, although they lacked the most important piece of the puzzle. They had not mastered people skills, which are critical in building a strong team. As you read this book, you'll find that Managers are only as good as the people who work for them.

It is my goal to influence managers to become people-oriented by treating their employees as their greatest asset. They are an investment, like stocks on Wall Street, which you have to monitor and manage in a delicate manner. It's similar to a marriage, or a spouse that you have made a commitment to. You constantly strive to improve it and don't give up easily.

Too often employees are taken for granted. With constant turnover, it becomes expensive to replace them, and you will rarely have trained personnel. Rather than spinning your wheels having to train new employees on a regular basis, try spending more time training, motivating, and developing the ones you already have.

From 1984 through 2004 I managed countless employees. To strengthen my knowledge, I've taken courses in business management and human relation skills. In addition to extensive experience and education, I had a wide variety of management training from on-the-job courses and seminars.

The task of managing employees is a never-ending challenge, and I was never bored. At times I managed as many as one hundred employees on a given day. That could have been one hundred different personalities, and it was my job to figure out what motivated each of them. It was also my job to understand one hundred different people's work ethics and their habits in the workplace. I had to determine how much supervision each employee required, as some required minimal and others required continuous supervision. The only way I knew was to observe each employee closely.

I joined the management, not primarily for the extra money, but to make a difference in the organization. I saw the way employees were being treated and thought there was a great deal of room for improvement. So . . . I decided to "bite the bullet" and pursue a management career. It was my goal to create a positive change in the company. I worked hard at treating employees the same way I wanted to be treated. I focused on rewarding employees who performed well and worked with employees to improve negative attitudes and unsatisfactory performance. I built a "team" of employees who took pride in their work, had positive attitudes, and improved productivity. It was a success, and I would like to take the time to share the knowledge I've gained, through my personal experiences, with you.

As you continue to read further, enjoy the humor and honesty of my own experiences from my management career spanning over twenty years. I am sure you will be able to relate to many of the situations I describe, and will find this information useful.

Experience in Management:

Manager of Customer Service	= 7 years
District Manager in Retail	= 5 years
Store Manager in Retail	= 6 years
Assistant Manager in Retail	= 1 year
Manager of a Car Wash	= <u>1 year</u>

{Owner of a Business for 8 Years}

20 years

COMPETITION
"PIECE OF THE PIE"

A Business World is Like a Pie

Every company wants to grab a piece of the pie. Matter of fact, each company wants to get the largest piece of the pie, if not all of the pie. The pie is the sales and profits of the organization. The pie begins whole, and as companies invade the pie with quality products, quality managers, quality sales staff, and a quality production line, the pie gradually gets eaten away. This is called the competition. An organization has the option to take the whole pie, 25 percent, 50 percent, or 75 percent. Companies ultimately make their own decision on how much of the pie they are willing to share with their competitors.

> The better the sales force . . .
> The better the production line . . .
> The better the production crew . . .
> The better the management staff . . .
> The bigger piece of the pie you will get!

Wouldn't it be great if you could have the whole pie, consisting of all the sales and profit in your industry? Keep in mind that the customer's pocketbook is the filling in the pie, and the portion of the pie you get depends on the quality of SERVICE you provide.

Customer Service must be #1 if you will receive the majority of the pie!

Why Do Companies Struggle to Be Profitable?

Company profits are directly related to how the organization treats its employees. If employees enjoy their job, they will be productive. If they are treated fairly, they will be less likely to call in sick when they are not ill. If they respect their manager, they will be willing to put forth the extra effort without being asked. If employees are satisfied with the job and their boss, they are likely to remain stable, which reduces turnover and training costs. If employees are treated as adults, they will act maturely and handle themselves in a professional manner.

If employees respect their manager, they will be willing to put forth the extra effort without being asked.

A sign on the door of a one-man business said . . .

CLOSED DUE TO ILLNESS
Sick of Work—Gone Fishing!

This sign represents how employees might feel on the job

How Do You Improve Employee Morale?

* Treat employees fairly and be honest with them.
* Create a "give and take" environment.
* Build mutual respect between the manager and employees.
* Be friendly and take a personal interest in them.
* Get to know your employees.
* Find out what motivates each employee.
* Recognize improvement, and employees who excel.
* Be "human" and allow others to be "human" as well.
* Set realistic goals that are achievable.
* Confront poor performers, the "Superstars" appreciate it.
* Be an effective communicator, squash rumors.
* As a leader, project a positive attitude.

IT WILL BE CONTAGIOUS!

By following these basic steps . . . it will reduce expenses and increase profit.

<u>INCREASE REVENUE</u>

Trained Staff
Safe Workplace
Productivity Goals
Effective Managers
Clean Environment
Qualified Sales Staff
Effective Leadership
Correct Poor Performance
Rewards and Recognition Issued

$$ EARNED = $$ SAVED = PROFIT $$$
$$ SAVED = $$ EARNED = PROFIT $$$

<u>REDUCE EXPENSES</u>

Save On Utilities
Reduce Overhead
Manage Effectively
Monitor Productivity
Consolidate Departments
Prevent Wasteful Spending
Eliminate Duplicate Processes
Eliminate Time-Wasting Practices
Only Purchase Necessities, Not Luxuries
Don't Be Too Quick to Sign the Blank Check!

MANAGER'S REPORT CARD

Self-Evaluation

Before you continue to read this book, take the time to complete the enclosed report card, to rate yourself in the management categories listed. This will assist you in a self-evaluation, to determine the areas that you have room to improve upon in your management skills. The report card is divided into six basic categories that you utilize on a daily basis, to be an effective manager. As you complete the report card, be honest with yourself to help you achieve the maximum benefit. Complete the report card with a black pen and keep it in a safe location.

After you have completely read this book, allow yourself ninety days to utilize the skills you learned. At the end of ninety days complete the report card again, with a red pen, and notice the difference in your management style. I'm confident that if you practice the skills you learned from reading this book, *you will be a more effective manager!*

Categories include:

I. Human Relation Skills
II. Supervision
III. Communication
IV. Problem Solving
V. Motivation
VI. Job Knowledge

MANAGER'S
REPORT CARD
FOR

————————————————————
NAME

Self-Evaluation
(Be honest with yourself)

1st Date Completed: _____

2nd Date Completed: _____

I.   HUMAN RELATION SKILLS:

	XLNT	ACCPTBLE	UNACC
1) Treats employees with respect	_____	_____	_____
2) Treats employees fairly	_____	_____	_____
3) Straightforward, honest approach	_____	_____	_____

II. SUPERVISION:

	XLNT	ACCPTBLE	UNACC
1) Coordinates work, gives direction as required	_____	_____	_____
2) Checks with employees to update progress	_____	_____	_____
3) Follows up in a timely manner	_____	_____	_____

III. COMMUNICATION:

XLNT ACCPTBLE UNACC

1) Keeps employees
   informed   _____   _____   _____

2) Encourages
   feedback from
   employees   _____   _____   _____

3) Listens to concerns
   and ideas   _____   _____   _____

IV. PROBLEM SOLVING:

XLNT ACCPTBLE UNACC

1) Able to make
   decisions   _____   _____   _____

2) Handles problem
   situations in a
   timely manner   _____   _____   _____

3) Follows up to
   resolve problem   _____   _____   _____

V. <u>MOTIVATION:</u>

	XLNT	ACCPTBLE	UNACC
1) Gives positive feedback	_____	_____	_____
2) Identifies employee potential/talent	_____	_____	_____
3) Creates a self-motivated work environment	_____	_____	_____

VI. <u>JOB KNOWLEDGE:</u>

	XLNT	ACCPTBLE	UNACC
1) Aware of policies and procedures	_____	_____	_____
2) Understands job requirements supervised	_____	_____	_____
3) Knowledge of company goals	_____	_____	_____

THE MANAGER

Chapter 1

TOPICS
CHAPTER 1
The Manager

* As a Manager . . .

* Styles of Management—Going to the Dogs!

* The "Maintenance Manager" Versus the "Mover and Shaker"

* Effective or Ineffective Managers

* Team Concept

* Human Relation Skills

* Mastering Listening Skills

* Challenging your Employees

* Micro-manager, Intimidator, Autocratic Boss

* Maintaining Control of the Workplace

* Managing the Stress of Management

* You are only as good as the employees who work for you

AS A MANAGER . . . you are the leader, you set the tone and you set the pace.

If you handle yourself in a professional manner, it will encourage your employees to be professional. If you set a fast pace, it will be contagious and spread to others. Be the example, so others will follow in your footsteps. Be consistent, so as not to confuse your employees.

---Webster's Definition---

LEADER:
A person or thing that leads, directing or commanding. A guiding head of a group.

LEADERSHIP:
The position or guidance of a leader. The ability to lead.

MANAGEMENT STYLES
Going to the Dogs!

Pit Bull Manager:
>   This dog charges and is trained to attack.
>   Pit bulls are protective of their territory.
>   Comes on strong, can intimidate by appearance.
>   Appears they go to the gym daily to work out.
>   Pit bulls project a "don't mess with me" attitude.
>   Give a dirty look when you enter in their space.

Poodle Manager:
>   A soft and gentle pup.
>   Poodles are loving and attach to their owner.
>   Go with the flow, easy going personality.
>   Poodles bark a lot, but never scare anyone.
>   Enjoy a walk in the park, when its not raining.

Labrador Retriever Manager:
>   Lab is well liked and friendly.
>   Smart animal and knows its place in the home.
>   Labs are caring, build a relationship with owner.
>   Assertive, but not too aggressive.
>   Protective of their owner and the property.
>   Will retrieve the morning paper if you request.
>   A Lab will not be taken advantage of.
>   They aren't afraid of others, but won't let anyone
>   take advantage of them.

So . . . which dog do you want to be known as?

THE "MAINTENANCE MANAGER"
Versus
THE "MOVER AND SHAKER"

Maintenance Manager:
- * Comfortable with productivity the way it is.
- * Doesn't challenge the workforce to improve.
- * Sees change as disruptive to the workplace.
- * Maintains the "status quo," business as usual.
- * Accepts the current level of productivity.
- * Does not strive to improve the process.

Mover and Shaker:
- * Has an assertive approach.
- * Enjoys a changing environment.
- * Builds confidence in employees.
- * Displays energy and moves in high gear.
- * Challenges employees to perform better.
- * Challenges one's self to attain higher goals.
- * Sets a higher goal and strives to achieve it.
- * Doesn't need a boss to direct or motivate them.
- * Finds creative and new ways to motivate.
- * Not reluctant to experiment with new ideas.

Do not wait for change to happen on its own. The "Mover and Shaker" will create their own change.

What category . . .

Does your management style fall into?
Would you prefer to be placed in as a manager?
Will achieve you the greatest success?
Would you place Bill Gates and Donald Trump in?

Why do companies need more "Mover and Shaker" managers? The answer is simple, since every organization must continually strive to remain competitive. If companies don't change with the times, they will eventually become sinking dinosaurs. In other words, their ship will sink with the times! Every organization has opportunities to improve their process as well as their productivity levels. Every company must find better and more cost-effective ways to conduct business. There isn't one organization that has enough "Mover and Shaker" managers.

You too ... can be a "Mover and Shaker"!

EFFECTIVE OR INEFFECTIVE MANAGERS
Who's who?

As a manager for over twenty years, I've had some excellent leaders to work for, and some that left a lasting impression (I'll never forget). I have gained knowledge from every one of them. By their example, the effective leaders taught me what worked well, and on the other hand, the ineffective leaders displayed what didn't work. I've worked for more than my share of managers. In my opinion, the business world has too many untrained and unqualified managers that lack the most important quality, people skills. Many employees I've spoke with feel this way, and would love to see a positive change in their boss. I have not only learned through my management career what works and what doesn't, I learned a variety of management styles and approaches.

One of the BEST managers I worked for . . .was encouraging, allowed me to be innovative, and try new ideas. They gave compliments when I performed well or exceeded their expectations. They were honest when I made a mistake, and then showed me the proper way. They were patient and allowed me a reasonable amount of time to become proficient at a task. They never held a grudge, they corrected my mistake and moved on! They gave me reasonable goals and expectations, that I was capable of attaining. They supported me when I made decisions, that I was confident would achieve a positive result. Finally, they challenged me to perform at a high level, and increased my company knowledge to further my career.

One of the worst managers I worked for . . .rarely complimented anyone and never thought the results were good enough. They generally focused on the negatives, and overlooked the positives. They didn't provide feedback (either positive or negative). I never knew where I stood, or what they thought of anyone's performance. They were moody most of the time, so I avoided them quite often to avoid confrontation. They had poor communication skills and rarely shared information so it was up to me to inquire. They limited my creativity, and preferred to make all the plans and decisions. They were rarely supportive of the decisions I made, without providing any feedback as to the reason why.

The business world has too many untrained, unqualified managers which lack the most important quality; PEOPLE SKILLS.

TEAM CONCEPT
Without a doubt,
It is proven that a team concept is the most effective

Football: The quarterback can't be effective without the offense. The runner can't catch a pass without the offensive players to block the other team. A touchdown can't be achieved without players to clear the path to the goal line.

Baseball: The batter can't hit the ball without the pitcher throwing it. The second baseman can't get the runner out without the outfielders. The catcher can't get the runner out without the infield.

Soccer: The team cannot prevent a goal without the goalie blocking the ball. A player can't pass the ball without the other team players. The better team will not win if they don't work together.

Basketball: A basketball team might not make a basket without a point guard. The team can't achieve a dunk without enough seven-foot players. They can't have a takeover without other team members to intercept the ball.

Volleyball: The front line can't survive without a setter to place the ball. A server needs players to encourage them so it won't be a net ball. The team can't survive without enough players.

A management team must have managers who are

willing to work together to achieve a common goal. It is necessary that they help each other to succeed, as well as respect one another. They must develop mutual trust, and cannot be reluctant to share their knowledge and experiences with the rest of the team members. In other words, they must "be on the same page" so they will be able to work together.

It's no secret that a team is more effective than any one individual. A protest has the greatest impact with a large group of people. The larger the group, the greater the impact will be. Unions are the most effective with a large membership, and you will find that stronger unions have the largest memberships. Attorneys are more effective in a group or team, to discuss the issues prior to a court hearing. The larger the team, the more input and feedback you receive.

So . . . does it make sense that a team of managers and employees will be more effective? When you evaluate what contributes to a company's success you will generally find a team concept in place. The phrase "the more the merrier" can be applied to the team concept. "The more the merrier" will achieve greater results!

You CANNOT afford to <u>not</u> work as a team!

HUMAN RELATION SKILLS
Also known as "People Skills"

In the management ranks you will hear a great deal about "human relation skills," so let us take the time to break this down:

Human: You must be "human" and treat others as they would like to be treated, with dignity and respect. Be responsive to an employees' needs, at work and at home. Consider the employees' feelings and listen to their concerns. Be sincere.

Relation: It is important to build positive relations with the employees you supervise. Get along with them. This does not mean that you have to be their personal friend outside of work. It is essential that you build mutual respect with all your employees, even the ones you clash with, and it must start with you, their leader. Get to know your employees, and find out what motivates each of them.

Skills: A skill is something you acquire and master. It is a talent that you develop, which helps you to perform a task. Having strong human relation skills is key to the successful management of your employees. If you are able to manage your employees, build and maintain strong relationships, you will be a successful manager. Managers with strong human relation skills are generally followed by employees who respect their leaders.

To sum it up, human relations (having strong people skills) will surround you with motivated employees who will want the organization to succeed, and it will make your job easier. It will also assist you in correcting employees with poor work habits. It will benefit you to understand an individual's personal issues that could be affecting their work performance. Finally, strong people skills will improve your communication and interaction with employees.

Ask yourself two simple questions:

1) Are your employees intimidated by you?

2) Do your employees respect you?

If you answered Yes to #1 or No to #2,
   you have room to improve on your
   human relation skills.

The better the PEOPLE SKILLS, The better the manager!

MASTERING
LISTENING SKILLS

It becomes necessary for managers to take an interest and show concern for their employees and their problems. Their concerns could be work related, such as a co-worker relationship or job stress. Their concerns could be personal, such as a marital relationship or financial hardship. The bottom line is, if an employee feels the need to share their concerns with you, it's a must that you take the time out of your busy day to talk with them. This might be the only opportunity that they give you. This will also send a message that you take a personal interest in them, and is extremely important in maintaining positive morale and productivity. As a manager you are not only their leader, you become their mentor and counselor. It is your duty to get them back on track as soon as possible so they will remain an asset to the company, and continue to be productive.

Some situations you will have control over and others you won't. Listen to your employees and be cautious of becoming too involved in their personal lives. It is not in your best interest to give advice regarding personal issues (relationships, finances, etc.). For non-work-related issues, refer the employee to a professional in the field, such as a counselor, attorney, financial advisor, or member of the clergy.

Get involved, get specifics, acquire statements, get the facts straight, discuss the issues with your fellow managers, and lay out a plan of action. Stay focused on the work-related issues and research what is going on with the employee.

Don't be rushed or distracted while the employee is sharing information with you, since various topics might need to be discussed in private. It never hurts to ask the employee if they need privacy.

If you don't show an interest in what the employee has to say, the silent message will be "You don't care." It's not only important for you to take an interest, it is critical that you react promptly to their concerns. Take the necessary time to research the employee's concerns and verify validity prior to acting on them. React promptly, don't overreact!

Always be sincere and honest with your employees so that you will build mutual respect for one another. If you are not able to assist the employee with their concerns, be sure to let them know in a timely manner.

Don't leave an employee hanging in the breeze, or they could blow away.

If you do not show an interest in your employees, the silent message will be "You don't care."

CHALLENGING YOUR EMPLOYEES
Workplace Challenge Falls into Two Categories

1) Find out which employees need to be challenged to perform better.

2) Find out which employees are interested in more of a challenge, possibly an increase in responsibility.

Be cautious not to force added responsibility onto those employees who are not interested. Identify employees that are interested and utilize them. Forcing an employee will likely cause decreased morale, followed by negative results. How will you know who might be interested? Simple . . . ask! If an employee tries added responsibilities, observe their actions and respond accordingly. Keep an eye on their body language, since it will tell a story.

Recognize bored and frustrated employees, as these behaviors could be signs that an employee might need a new assignment or new challenge. Communicate with them regularly and you will find out. An employee who becomes sidetracked easily could be showing a sign of boredom that could lead to trouble down the road. Inquire about the cause, since it could be a personal issue affecting their work. Bored employees are at a high risk of becoming a problem. This concept is similar to bored teenagers who could lose focus and travel down the wrong path. A bored employee could become your next union representative, working against the management. Utilize bored employees to your advantage, by delegating special projects to them. By delegating, it will allow you more time to effectively manage your employees.

As a manager, it is your primary responsibility to observe your employees every day; to include their work habits, behaviors, productivity, actions, reactions, as well as their body language. This sounds like a lot of work, but it's really not. You shouldn't remain in your office any more than is absolutely necessary. The more time you spend in your office away from your employees, the less time you will have to observe them performing the work.

And . . .

that will be a detriment to your organization.

You can't afford that expense!

MICRO-MANAGER, INTIMIDATOR, AUTOCRATIC BOSS

The Boss You Don't Want To Be...

<u>Micro-Manager:</u> Micro-Managers generally have a lack of confidence in their employees. They feel their employees don't have a mind of their own, and are never as smart as they are. They look over their employees' shoulder continuously, treat them as if they are still new hires, and feel a need to create all the new programs. They give the impression to their employees that they aren't responsible enough to work without supervision. They have a tendency to irritate the productive workers and stifle employee creativity.

<u>Intimidator:</u> The Intimidator has a bold and aggressive style. It is an "in your face" approach. These managers don't allow employees to have any space of their own. This management style might achieve short-term results, although it commonly backfires on managers in the long term. They are demanding, have unreasonable expectations, and will break down a team effort, while causing animosity. They will de-motivate employees and send morale spiraling downward.

<u>Autocratic Boss:</u> The Autocratic Boss is similar to a dictator. Such managers are not tactful and are very demanding. They are blunt in their approach, using phrases such as "just do it," or "get it done". They might require the employee to address them as "Ma'am" or "Sir" to show respect. They have a ten-

dency to demand the employee's respect, rather than earn it, and they rarely get it. They are not good for a unit that is struggling to improve productivity.

As a manager, you want to be a leader who sets the example.

MAINTAINING CONTROL OF THE WORKPLACE

WITHOUT BEING TOO OBVIOUS

Are the employees in control, or is the manager in control? Is the "Union" in control of the company and the workers? We know that it better be the manager. There are no ifs, ands, or buts about it.

If the manager is not in control of the workplace, that could be similar to a haunted house on Halloween night; quite a scary situation! Take control by setting goals, expectations, and limits for employees. Once you have established them, it is necessary that you follow up regularly. Follow up is the key to achieving success, and it must be ongoing. When you stop the follow up process, the results tend to stop improving.

Being in control of your unit does not mean being a dictator or a ruler. It means being a role model, setting the tone, and setting the pace for your employees to work at. If you choose to be a dictator or a ruler, the risks of failure drastically increase. When you were the employee working for your manager, what type of manager did you prefer to work for . . . The Dictator, The Ruler, The Pace Setter, or the Role Model?

Without a doubt, I would rather work for a manager that is reasonable, fair, and is a positive role model. When you were a child, what type of leader or parent did you prefer . . . The Dictator, The Ruler, or the positive Role Model? This same logic applies in the workplace.

In a manager's role you do not want it to become too obvious that you are in control. Do not advertise it on the company bulletin board, or a billboard in the parking lot! Be subtle about it, and it will be more effective.

Being in control includes the following managerial traits:

1) Respect for employees as well as upper-level management.

2) Utilization of support resources, such as manuals or departments.

3) Utilization of reference tools, such as policies and training material.

4) Become a knowledgeable manager; ask questions.

5) Always maintain integrity; be trustworthy.

6) Maintain ongoing follow up, never saying you are *too busy*; make the time for it.

MANAGING THE STRESS
OF MANAGEMENT
By . . .

Organizing yourself, Communicating expectations,
Delegating the workload, Following Up

Managing employees does not have to be as stressful as
many managers allow it to be. That is not to say that it will
not be stressful at times. It is how you react to the stress
that will make the difference. I have found that there are
roughly 10–20 percent of employees in the average workforce that tend to create added stress for the manager. Do
you allow your employees to "get under your skin," and
then advertise it? Or do you make it invisible?

As a manager, when you increase your knowledge
and experience, your stress level will be reduced. You do
have control over how much stress you allow yourself to
be under, and you also have control over how you let it
affect your job.

In addition to unproductive, uncooperative employees, the way your upper-level management communicates
with you could affect your stress level. Self-imposed
stress can also be caused by:

> * Lack of experience in the job
> * Lack of people skills
> * Lack of technical knowledge

How can you reduce your stress level? Make the time
to take courses offered by your employer or sign up for a

night class on human relation skills. Be willing to learn from others, observe successful managers, and utilize what already works. Don't be afraid to solicit feedback or ask for new ideas.

YOU ARE ONLY AS GOOD AS THE EMPLOYEES WHO WORK FOR YOU ...

Employees will either make you shine or make you look like "Ivan the Terrible." They will lead you to success or failure, and will play a major role in your personal success within the organization. Your primary focus as a manager MUST be to develop your employees. It is physically impossible for you to do all of the work, so it becomes necessary to hire qualified people who are trainable.

You MUST discover ways to empower your employees to maximize productivity. You MUST create a positive work environment so your employees won't mind coming to work and will work hard. You MUST supply the necessary tools and equipment for employees to perform the tasks. You MUST communicate expectations and goals in a simple manner so they are clearly understood by everyone. You MUST identify and correct poor performance. If you fail to do so, performance will not improve. You MUST recognize and reward excellence. Rewarding good workers with additional work is not a reward! Verbal or monetary recognition is appropriate; that will encourage results.

Building a team is critical to your unit. Everyone MUST work together to achieve the common goals. A team will share ideas, and work together to increase revenue and reduce expenses.

Keep in mind that your customers are your paycheck, and without them no one would be paid. Customers fill up the bank account and they will not return if they are not satisfied with the product or service they receive.

<u>Consider the following qualities when selecting
individuals to be on your team:</u>

Are you choosing people . . .

Who are goal oriented?
Who have a high energy level?
Who adapt well to change?
Who appear to be quick learners?
Who display a strong work ethic?
Who show an interest in the company?
Who demonstrate good common sense?
Who have innovative ideas and creative skills?
Who have the qualities to eventually replace you?
Who believe in all of the company products to sell?

Are you choosing people who truly believe that
THE CUSTOMER IS ALWAYS #1?

*The quality of your team determines the quality of
YOU, the manager.*

POINTS TO REMEMBER

The Manager / Chapter 1

A Successful Manager
will NOT make excuses,

rather,
they WILL find ways to
get the job done!

Finally . . .

finish reading this book,

remember what you read,

and

Put the information to use!

THE
EMPLOYEE

Chapter
2

TOPICS

Chapter 2
The Employee

* Work Ethic

* Employee Profiles

* Personalities

* Managing Employees Can Be Like a Three-Ring Circus

* Perceptions Are Greater Than the Truth

* Superstar Employee

* Employees Who Work Harder at NOT working

* Slug! What Type of Employee Is This?

* Consequences to Poor Work Habits

* Life's Not Fair! So . . . Get Used to It!

* Morale in the Workplace

WORK ETHIC

Everyone's work ethic varies, and is generally influenced by their background and experiences. Work ethics are shaped by the following factors:

* Family—Parents, Grandparents, Aunts, Uncles, Siblings
* Religious—Clergy
* Peers—Friends, Co-workers
* Teachers—Primary School, College
* Employer—Previous Manager
* Yourself—Pride

My father was my strongest influence. He was a workaholic. He worked hard to provide for the family, since my mother was a stay-at-home mom. My mother raised the four children and my father worked well into his mid-seventies.

Create your own standards for excellence and strive to achieve it daily. Set your own personal goals that are challenging and realistic. When I wrote this book while working full time, I set a timeline to complete the writings as well as the publishing. By setting these goals and staying focused, I attained them. It is possible for you to have a direct influence on an employee's work ethic. People continue to have influences throughout their entire life that will shape and reshape their work ethic. Generally, the older that people get, they become set in their ways. But that does not mean an individual's work ethic cannot change. It might be necessary to become more patient with people as they age. Some people will strongly resist change, and others will rebel against it.

Q: **How can a manager influence an employee's work ethic?**

A: **Set the pace and be an example of what you expect.**

Work ethic is a "base" for a level of performance. Effective leaders will breed a strong work ethic and it will be contagious. Keep in mind that a leader is not just a parent or a teacher, it is also the employer. The average person will spend approximately 33 percent of their time at work, 33 percent asleep, and 33 percent at home as a leader for their family.

So . . . who really influences 33 percent of an employee's day?

It's YOU . . . the manager!

Strong Work Ethic
=
Strong Leaders

"Base" For An Average Work Ethic

Poor Leaders
=
Poor Work Ethic

EMPLOYEE PROFILES
First Impressions

How often does a first impression influence your perception of what an employee's work ethic will be? As the saying goes, appearance is not everything, and appearance doesn't always tell the entire story. As a manager I have experienced this on several occasions. To protect the individuals' names from being used, I've come up with false names to describe the various types of employees I managed. These employees proved me wrong about their work habits. Their appearance was questionable, although each employee performed the work of two people.

Mr. Rough : Mr. "Rough" was a bit rough looking around the edges. He had shoulder-length hair and a scruffy beard that was a bit long, and wore dark sunglasses. He kept warm with a black leather jacket and rode to work on a Harley Davidson motorcycle. His Harley was always polished so that it sparkled. Mr. Rough spoke with a deep voice that carried across the room. But . . . he was a very hard worker!

Mr. Worker : Mr. "Worker" was your average person by appearance. He wasn't muscular, or a "Slim Jim," by any means. But, he was hyper and had a great deal of energy. He would go non-stop all day long and not run low on energy. Mr. Worker was productive, at a fast pace, and set the tone for his co-workers.   And . . . he would always complete the task ahead of schedule!

Mr. Senior : Mr. "Senior" was over fifty-five years old when he began working for me, and he was in excellent physical condition. You could tell that Mr. Senior ate a lot of vegetables and got his regular share of exercise. He was full of energy, even in the early morning hours before sunrise. He was experienced, with a lot of knowledge and great ideas. Mr. Senior had been "around the block" a few times and knew his stuff. Remember . . . don't take him for granted!

Looks aren't everything . . . don't judge by appearances alone.

PERSONALITIES

Many authors and psychologists have divided various personality types by using the A, B, C method. Type "A" is this, and type "B" is that. I do not see personalities like the alphabet, rather I describe them as being associated with specific traits:

Approachable	Humorous	Serious
Assertive	Introverted	Shy
Aggressive	Obnoxious	Unapproachable
Extroverted	Personable	Unfriendly
Friendly	Reserved	Wild
Goofy	Rude	Witty

Most personalities are mixed with a combination of at least six traits. Sometimes you will get "blackjack" and at times you will "bust"! When interviewing and selecting your team, determine what personality traits your prospect has, and how they will fit best with your team.

The make-up of your team should combine various types of personalities. To be an effective organization, you will need a variety of personalities for the different types of jobs you will assign. It will not take the same personality type for a sales position as it will for an accountant. One needs to be outgoing and the other could be shy, yet both employees can be effective in their position. Always match the job description with the personality traits. It requires different personalities for various responsibilities, such as a manager versus an employee. An employee can be the reserved type, and the manager needs to be the assertive type.

MANAGERS = Assertive, Approachable, Extroverted, Friendly, Humorous, Observant, Personable, Serious, Witty

MANAGING EMPLOYEES

Can Be Like a Three-Ring Circus

<u>The Clown:</u> This employee is truly the Joker! The employee is rarely serious at work, and does a good job overall. Clowns love to draw attention to themselves. The clown can be disruptive at times, can liven up the group, and usually a joy to have around. They keep the workplace lively, although sometimes a bit too lively.

<u>The Entertainer:</u> This employee loves to be on stage telling jokes to co-workers, and doesn't pick good times to perform. Entertainers work on drawing a large crowd, hoping to be a sell-out. They enjoy talking, and at times will talk too much, disrupting productivity. They get distracted easily, which will prevent them from completing a task on time. Entertainers are often time wasters, so you might need to supervise them closely. Remember, their priority is to be entertaining!

<u>The Tightrope Walker:</u> Tightrope Walkers know their limits (the edge), and know when they are about to fall off of the rope. They will challenge their leader on occasion, will be assertive, and will take risks that most employees will not take. In a unionized work environment, they will interpret the union contracts effectively. They generally know the policies and their rights under the union contract better than most of your employees. Be aware . . . the Tightrope Walker is not shy!

<u>The Ringleader:</u> The Ringleader might be your next union representative. This is the "leader of the pack" and might follow a sign of trouble. Ringleaders might attempt to break up the team you worked hard to create. They might even build their own team, and possibly tear down and destroy the rest of your group. The Ringleader knows how to "work the system" to their advantage. This employee will spend time studying the manuals so they will be knowledgeable of the rules and regulations, as well as their own personal rights. The Ringleader can be disruptive to the workplace and dislikes a changing environment.

<u>The Elephant:</u> These employees will be the best for your team, as they remain focused and know where they are going at all times. The elephant follows orders, generally listens to the master, and the elephant is not disruptive to the rest of their group. They usually follow good workers and go with the flow. Elephants are smart and compliant.

You will want to have as many elephants on your team as possible.

PERCEPTIONS

Are GREATER Than The Truth

Believe it or not . . . you will be surprised how true this is! The way that your employees perceive you as a manager has a great impact on the respect they give you. An employee's perception can be true or false, although they will have a strong belief that what they feel is true. It is not easy to change one's perception of you, as a manager, once you've convinced them what you are all about.

Each employee is unique in their own way, and could perceive you differently. They might feel that you have ulterior motives or they might not feel confident that they can trust you. They could be wondering what is in it for you, as the manager. Employees might interpret your message differently. Again it is how they perceive it that is important. Managers in general do not spend time trying to understand how their employees perceive them, their intentions, or their goals. To minimize misunderstandings, it becomes necessary to be specific and give detailed explanations when communicating to your employees. Keep the information short and to the point. This will keep the employees' attention and prevent the message from becoming boring. You must hold their attention to maintain the employees' focus, and always recap the highlights from your meeting.

Don't expect every employee to respond the same way. Their perception of the message will play a role in their response. A person's response is triggered by their perception.

SUPERSTAR"
Employee

Don't Burn Out Your Superstars

All managers have top-notch employees who they categorize as their Superstar employees. Be careful not to abuse these workers. It is not uncommon for managers to utilize these employees to pick up the slack for the ones that are not being productive. This is clearly the wrong approach. Take on the challenge to correct poor performance, as described in my next book (Management S.O.S.—"Improving Performance"), rather than unloading extra work on your great employees. Your Superstars will quickly become disgusted with those that do not carry their weight. They will also get fed up with the manager, if they are required to pick up the slack for others. The Superstars could be carrying the company or the unit you supervise. Do not abuse them or you will lose them from your team.

Hire, train, and motivate as many employees as you can to become Superstars. The more you have on your team, the more successful you will be as a manager. Some Superstars were born that way and some are molded by parents, teachers, religious leaders, and employers. As a manager, you play a major role in developing Superstars.

Treat your Superstars well, encourage positive behavior, and they will continue to produce for you. Recognize and reward their efforts, and be sincere or it will not count. Show your appreciation for a job well done and verbally thank them for their contribution.

YOU too can be a "Superstar Manager."

Don't abuse your "Superstars" or you will lose them from the team.

EMPLOYEES WHO WORK HARDER AT NOT WORKING,

Than Actually Working At All

A small percentage of employees (less than 10 percent) spend more time discovering ways to get out of work than they spend actually doing the work. These employees are constantly looking for ways to get out of working. They will search for the loopholes to free themselves from the four-letter word "WORK." They know their rights as well as the rules and regulations. Work is not a pleasant thing for them.

So . . . why do these employees still expect a paycheck? Isn't the paycheck supposed to be a trade-off for productive work? Unfortunately, not with their mentality! I always thought it was a trade-off before I decided to join the management ranks, and I believe the same concept exists today. These employees have developed poor work habits along the way, have become lazy, and management has allowed it to continue. These employees have gotten into this routine and believe that their level of performance is acceptable.

Why doesn't it change?
Because management does not
require it to!

What can a manager do to correct this behavior?

1) Challenge employees to do their best.
2) Set specific performance expectations.
3) Hold them accountable for performance.
4) Find out what motivates each employee.
5) Don't wait for perfection, recognize progress.
6) Ask employees about their goals, help them achieve them.

"SLUG"

Have You Ever Seen A "Slug" On The Move?

Most managers have at least one S-L-o-o-o-w employee on their workforce. Approximately 10–20 percent of the workforce could be "Slugs." Through my twenty years of experience I found that 80–90 percent of employees do not require much supervision. The remaining 10–20 percent is where those Slugs could be found, and you should not have to look very hard. They can be found in the "spotlight," and will raise their hand often to get attention. They claim that they forget the policies or procedures, which will make them easily recognized. Why are these employees nicknamed "Slugs"? It has to do with the pace they work at. They could be close to retirement, have a broken-down body, lack motivation, or be tired, distracted at work, lazy, or all of these. Ask yourself— Does this Slug have the potential to perform better? Is health, disability, or age affecting the employee's work? Why is this employee performing at such a slow pace? Have they been properly trained to perform the job? Is the employee utilizing all the available tools and support resources? Have any productivity goals or expectations been communicated to them? Who has spoken to them regarding their lack of performance?

The answers to these questions will help you determine if you have a true Slug on your hands, or if you just have a weak performer that needs grooming. A Slug does not have to remain a slug forever. They could become a "Spider" who works hard to build webs, or they could become an "Ant" who is always on the move!

CONSEQUENCES TO POOR WORK HABITS

As a manager, I've supervised numerous employees
who love to "test the water."

Is the water too hot or too cold? How much room will
you give an employee to be unproductive? The more that
you allow, the more they might take. Generally, this is
not true for the majority of employees, since my experience has shown that only an average of 10–20 percent of
workers act this way. If you do not have consequences to
negative behavior, there is a slim chance that it will improve on its own. Second and third consequences must be
more severe, issued in a progressive manner. Do not wait
too long to give a consequence to an employee. If there
are no consequences to poor behavior, you have silently
stated that it is acceptable. Improved work habits rarely
occur on their own. It becomes necessary to forewarn
employees of what the consequences to their behavior
will be. The forewarning process should get their attention in most cases, to change the negative behavior before
it escalates. It must never be a surprise to an employee
when they receive a consequence, and they should always
be verbally warned prior to the action taking place.

*When consequences do not exist, there is a slim
chance for improvement.*

LIFE'S NOT FAIR

So . . .
Get Used To It!

How often have you heard the phrase "life's not fair"?

More than likely you have heard this phrase more times than you can count. I lost count many years ago. This was one of my kids' most favorite phrases until I broke them of the habit. Over the years my children learned to avoid saying it, because they knew what my response would be. You guessed it . . .

"Life's not fair—so get used to it!"

Reality has proven that life will never be fair. Personal finances will never be fair and job status won't seem fair. This includes the compensation you will receive. Relationships with a spouse, partner, or family members might not be fair. And if you have siblings, life just won't seem fair! I have told this to my children, my friends, and my employees. Do not feel bad when you need to tell yourself that life's not fair, so get used to it!

As much as we like to think that we are in full control of our lives, we are not. I have experienced this firsthand when I had a boss that did not like me for whatever reason, and they built barriers around my advancement opportunities. On another occasion I became ill and had no control over the symptoms I endured, and had to be patient until I fully recovered. These are obstacles that most of us have to deal with at various stages of our life. We do not have to like the fact that life can be unfair, we just have to get used to it.

It is ok to inform your employees that some situations might not seem fair. Every attempt must be made by you, as their manager, to treat all employees in a fair manner. If an employee thinks that a decision or situation is unfair, take time to explain the reasoning for it. Employees might perceive you as being unfair, so be cognizant of the image you project to your staff. Be aware of the perceptions that employees might develop about you, as their leader. A manager's goal is to be as fair as possible with everyone.

As the saying goes . . .
"What's fair is fair, and what's not is not"!
Fairness will motivate employees and bring positive results.

MORALE IN THE WORKPLACE

Attitudes directly affect performance . . . Which directly affects productivity.

Morale is best explained as the enthusiasm you acquire toward performing the job, confidence you have in the task, and the courage you have to fulfill your job. Developing high morale is critical to your success as well as the company's success. Your long-term success depends on high morale. Short-term success is not as dependent on high morale. Your goal as a manager is to strive for long-term success which creates a "rock solid" company and plenty of job security for you, your peers, and the employees.

Morale follows an attitude. Positive attitudes lead to high morale and poor attitudes lead to poor morale. It is a manager's responsibility to influence attitudes in a positive manner, which will directly affect one's morale in the workplace.

Low morale brings poor performance, poor sales results, dissatisfied customers, upset suppliers, an increase in employee accidents and injuries, irregular attendance, and the risk of internal theft. It is no secret that your organization cannot afford to have low employee morale, and if it does, it will not remain in business very long.

High morale brings increased sales, increased productivity, satisfactory customer surveys, low accident and injury rates, and increased staffing (reduction in sick calls). There is no doubt that this is where a company must focus to increase profit and reduce expenses.

As a manager, your own morale will influence your employees' morale. Keep in mind that your employees see you as the leader. You are their role model, so, in other words . . . it is not an option for you to have anything less than high morale. The way employees perceive your morale will affect their perception of your attitude as well.

YOU CANNOT AFFORD TO HAVE LOW MORALE.

It's NOT an option!

An employee's work habits
are directly related
to their attitude.

Focus on improving
employee morale.

MANAGING EMPLOYEES

Chapter 3

TOPICS

Chapter 3
Managing Employees

RETURNING...

BACK TO BASICS

Managing employees breaks down into four basic categories:

TRAIN
MOTIVATE
DELEGATE
FOLLOW UP

If you practice these concepts, you WILL be a successful manager.

You will manage more effectively as you read further and put these basic steps to use.

You will be amazed at the results!

TRAIN – MOTIVATE – DELEGATE – FOLLOW UP

FOUR BASIC STEPS
TO EFFECTIVE SUPERVISION

I - Train: You must train the employee to be proficient at a task. Do not assume that the employee knows what you expect. Set your expectations for the employee based upon how well you have trained them for the assignment. You cannot hold them accountable if you haven't properly trained them.

Ask yourself—Was the employee properly and completely trained for the job?

II - Motivate: As a manager you must take an active role in motivating your employees. Create an environment where employees enjoy coming to work, since they spend much of their life there. Ask each employee (individually) what motivates them to work to their maximum potential, and find creative ways to motivate them. Recognize and reward positive performance and behaviors, and respond quickly to improve productivity. Be consistent and communicate effectively.

III – Delegate: Do not be afraid to delegate assignments or responsibilities to qualified individuals. Delegating will show employees that you are confident in their knowledge and ability. Delegating work to others will free a portion of your time and it will reduce your stress level. It will also challenge others to excel to the next level.

TRAIN – MOTIVATE – DELEGATE – FOLLOW UP

When delegating, you must review the work to ensure that it is complete and accurate. You are the person that is ultimately responsible for the work you delegate to others.

IV – Follow Up: You must follow up on the work to be sure that it meets your satisfaction. It is necessary to provide feedback to the employee on how well they performed the task. Encourage the employee and identify PROGRESS. Do not wait for perfection! Be sure to recognize the employee's effort and thank them for a job well done. If it is an ongoing project, provide periodic feedback to update them on their progress, and answer questions that they might have.

TRAIN – MOTIVATE – DELEGATE – FOLLOW UP

TRAINING
Training Employees Must Be A Top Priority
This will be your recipe for success!

RECIPE:
  Add
2 quarts of Knowledge
1 pint of Confidence
3 sheets of Material (to study)
4 pinches of Time (thyme)
1 teaspoon of Encouragement
½ cup of Follow Up and Feedback
Heat on low and check on frequently

As a manager you must rank training as number one. If you do not train thoroughly, you are not being fair to yourself or the company. It is impossible for you to do all of the work without burning out, so it is critical that you train your employees to assist you.

Some managers do not train their employees for additional assignments because they say it takes too much of their time. Unfortunately, some managers don't train because they are not confident in their people's ability to learn. These are all poor excuses. Training is time-consuming but it will be beneficial in the long term. You will need a trained and productive workforce, and that does not happen by luck! Training your employees builds confidence and will encourage them to succeed.

Lack of training on a manager's part will make the job more stressful. Some managers do not feel the need to train because they think they can do the job better or faster themselves. This type of management style is dangerous.

TRAIN – MOTIVATE – DELEGATE – FOLLOW UP

MOTIVATING

Different Strokes for Different Folks!

"Different strokes for different folks" is exactly what we, as managers, must do when recognizing the extra effort of employees. Each person is an individual, which means that each person is motivated differently. They might react differently, and could have different wants and needs. Two different people could be motivated in two completely different ways.

It is necessary to ask each employee what motivates them. Some of the answers might be . . .

* Pat on the back
* Verbal "thank you" (one-on-one)
* "Thank you" in a group
* Award or plaque
* Monetary reward
* Box of chocolates
* An inexpensive gift
* Preferred day off
* Overtime/extra hours
* Prize from a drawing
* Gift certificate
* Added responsibility
* Promotion
* Raise in pay
* Bonus $$$
* Thank-you card
* Get off work early
* NOTHING AT ALL!!

If you recognize positive results, including progress, it will generate continued positive behavior. If you don't recognize the positive, it could turn to negative results. Motivating your employees is essential to the success of your company.

TRAIN – MOTIVATE – DELEGATE – FOLLOW UP

YOU, as a manager, are the person responsible for motivating your employees.

You must spend the necessary time to motivate your employees. You have more influence over the motivation of your staff than you might realize. Some managers think that it is not possible to motivate employees, but do not be fooled. These managers are wrong! You have no control over your employees' personal life, but you have a great deal of control in the work environment. The way an employee feels on the job will directly affect their work. Your company style, approach, and policies can also motivate or de-motivate employees. You must look at what you, the manager, have control over and what you don't. If you have control over it, it is your job to improve it.

TRAIN – MOTIVATE – DELEGATE – FOLLOW UP

DELEGATING

In many companies the workload of a manager can be overwhelming. It might become necessary to ask yourself:

What options do I have? The answer is: Delegating assignments or projects to qualified individuals.

Questions:
1) Have I identified intelligent employees that are working for me?
2) Do I have any employees that are ready to be trained on a new task?
3) Which employees are interested in taking on additional responsibilities?
4) What tasks could I delegate and what should I accomplish myself?

The benefits of delegating outweigh those of the only other option; doing it all yourself. You will add unnecessary stress to your life by attempting to accomplish everything yourself. When you are overloaded, you might become irritable and impatient, which could create a sub-zero climate, and reduce productivity levels.

It is possible that you could lose the cooperative work environment you worked so hard to create. You could be locking up your undeveloped talent in a closet because you do not feel comfortable utilizing it. By delegating the paperwork or other projects, it will allow you more time to manage your employees. You should spend 80–90 percent of your day observing and managing the employees, and the remainder managing paperwork!

TRAIN – MOTIVATE – DELEGATE – FOLLOW UP

FIVE STEPS TO A SUCCESSFUL DELEGATOR

1) Do not be afraid to delegate work to others.
2) Ask, don't tell (do not be a Dictator).
3) Train the employee properly for the task.
4) Show appreciation for the completed work.
5) Provide feedback on the assignment.

Keep in mind that you, as the manager, have the authority to delegate tasks. When you assign a task, you are ultimately responsible for the end result. Follow up is critical, and always provide feedback for the employee. As companies strive to be the best, and increase profits, managers are continually asked to complete additional work with fewer resources. Delegating is often a necessity for managers, just like water and food. Being reluctant to delegate sends a negative message to employees that you do not have confidence in their abilities. This is not the message you want to be sending to your team.

TRAIN – MOTIVATE – DELEGATE – FOLLOW UP

FOLLOWING UP

As Managers...

How often do we implement new programs and forget to follow up to ensure they are fully implemented?

How often do we require employees to follow new procedures, without following up to be sure they are fully implemented?

How often do we set goals and give expectations to employees, without following up to ensure that the goals are being met?

How often do we show an employee a more efficient way to complete a task, without following up to be sure they complete the task as trained?

BEFORE YOU READ FURTHER,
RATE YOURSELF ON THE TASK OF
FOLLOW UP
(scale of 1–10, circle one)
1 2 3 4 5 6 7 8 9 10

You must take time out of your busy day for follow up. This is NOT optional if you intend to be an effective leader. It is beneficial to take notes of performance observations, to use as a reference on a future date. If you have no intention of following up, you are wasting your time setting goals, establishing policies, and giving instructions. Set your priorities on what rates an "A," then a "B," and so forth. Follow up on progress . . . and don't wait for completion in case the assignment might have to be re-done. Progress must be reviewed frequently, and depending upon the accuracy of the job, you might be able to reduce the frequency of the follow up process. Do not become too comfortable and eliminate the follow up altogether, or you might regret it. It is helpful to utilize a daily planning calendar, by noting the dates for future follow up sessions.

How many times have you asked . . .

Your kid to take out the trash?

Your child to clean their room?

Your spouse to please pay the bills?

Your partner to please run an errand?

An employee to clean up their work area?

A sales clerk to suggest an additional item/up-sell?

How many times have your requests been completely ignored?

Effective follow up will achieve dramatic results. The sooner the follow up process takes place, the sooner you see the results. The gaps between the goal and the actual will begin to close.

TRAIN – MOTIVATE – DELEGATE – FOLLOW UP

ACCOUNTABILITY

It goes without saying . . . accountability *WILL* lead to success!

Most work units have a desire and a need to increase accountability. It seems as if organizations are continually striving to increase accountability at all levels. This results in:

Increase in Profit
Remaining Competitive
Increase in Productivity
Stability and Job Security

Lack of accountability leads to a lack of results

TRAIN – MOTIVATE – DELEGATE – FOLLOW UP

EMPOWER YOUR EMPLOYEES

Defined in Webster's Dictionary:

EMPOWER – to give power or authority to; to authorize, as the president is empowered to veto legislation; to give ability to; enable, as science empowers men to control natural forces more effectively. Also spelled "Impower"; synonym to; authorize, license, commission, delegate, warrant

As managers, it is our job to empower our employees. This is not an easy task and can be quite a challenge. It will bring gratification when you successfully empower employees. Empowering your employees will lead to creating a positive attitude toward their job, and developing respect for their leader. When you have employees that are empowered, you will notice a significant difference in their attitude and behavior from your "Average Joe" employee. They will require minimal supervision, if any at all. They will take care of business in your absence, and you won't have a "workplace tornado" upon returning from a vacation.

Empowerment comes from you, their manager, so get your employees involved. Instill confidence in them, train people thoroughly, and be fair but equitable. Do not show favoritism. Successful empowerment will lead to a self-managed workforce, which most employees prefer. Treat your employees as adults, in a professional manner, and remember to acknowledge their level of intelligence. Utilize their knowledge and experience to become a more effective organization. Hopefully your employees were not hired for their lack of intelligence.

TRAIN – MOTIVATE – DELEGATE – FOLLOW UP

Develop and utilize their hidden talents, and encourage your employees to share new ideas to generate additional revenue. Challenge them to be creative, since everyone has special talents that they are stronger at than others. Some people are very organized, some are financial wizards, some have the quality of "sales gab," and some will have the "take charge" leadership qualities. It will benefit you to match their unique talents with the job that requires the qualities they have mastered.

There is an assignment for everyone. Have you determined what every one of your employees' unique quality is? If you haven't begun to, it is never too late to start. ***START NOW***!

As a manager, accept the fact that you do not know everything, and you will not have all of the answers to problems. Your employees are just as smart as you, so do not take them for granted, and be careful not to waste their hidden talents. The people who know how to do the job best are the ones who do it every day.

EMPOWER: Encourage and enable them to lead the way.

TRAIN – MOTIVATE – DELEGATE – FOLLOW UP

Is it really the manager who knows how to perform the work in the most efficient manner?

The answer is often: NO. Why is this true?

Too often managers make decisions for a work unit that they've never actually worked in. The best ideas commonly come from individuals that perform the work daily. They are the best resource to find out what works and what does not. It is beneficial for you to ask employees for their input on how to increase revenue and reduce expenses. Keep in mind that a manager will not have all of the answers. Be approachable and responsive to their input, and listen to suggestions. Do not hesitate to experiment with another individual's idea. It might be the best one you receive, to improve productivity or reduce expenditures. By asking for input and trying new ideas, you will build a stronger team to work toward achieving the goals. Too often, higher-ranking officials make decisions at headquarters that have a large impact on the workforce, without ever involving the employees who work in those operations. This could generate a negative reaction from employees, leading to decreased results.

How do we involve the employees who actually do the work?

TRAIN – MOTIVATE – DELEGATE – FOLLOW UP

1) Share the problems with employees and ask for solutions.
2) Ask what impact their solution will have on the problem.
3) Consider their input prior to finalizing a decision.
4) Discuss possible solutions with other managers, get opinions.
5) Consider your own solution and what impact it could have.
6) Analyze the various solutions to determine which one is best.
7) Make a final decision, and test the proposed solution.
8) Set up an evaluation process with a timeline.

Now you have gained a sense of confidence in your employees. You gave them an opportunity to be a part of the solution, not only a part of the problem. The ones who complain the most should be your first resource. You have now gotten your employees involved in the fix-it process, made them feel a part of the team, and let them know their opinion counts. They will be more apt to "buy in" to the process rather than rebel against it. If you select one of their ideas, your employees will feel a sense of ownership in the company. Your employees will take pride in their job, as if they have made a contribution. This will result in improved attitudes . . . followed by improved productivity . . . followed by reduced expenses . . . followed by an increase in profit . . . followed by a successful organization!

TRAIN – MOTIVATE – DELEGATE – FOLLOW UP

RESHAPING BEHAVIORS

A manager's responsibility is to focus on the behavior of the employees, not their personality traits. The specific work habits are the behaviors that must be addressed. By focusing on the personality, you will not achieve the results you desire. It is the behaviors that must change to improve productivity. Attitude usually affects behavior, although you must always remain focused on the actual behaviors that you desire to influence.

Reshaping behaviors becomes an investment like stocks and bonds. Just like a makeover, you are looking for a return on your investment. Invest in your employees; invest training, invest communication, invest in a positive role model, and finally, invest time. The larger the investment, the larger the potential return! It is a bit like gambling at the blackjack table or purchasing risky stocks. You will not win big unless you take a risk and increase your investment.

Replacing an employee will be an expensive financial burden to your company. That is not to say that you will not have to terminate employees from time to time, but first you must work hard at reshaping their behaviors, and do not give up too quickly. If you put forth the effort, most negative behaviors can be turned around. The majority of employees need and want their job. Some might not like their job or their boss, although they will need it for survival.

Set your expectations high for each individual and be sure they clearly understand them. *Don't accept less than you expect!* It is essential that you allow a reasonable time for employees to meet your expectations. Be realistic and set obtainable goals, so your employees will not feel overwhelmed and frustrated.

TRAIN – MOTIVATE – DELEGATE – FOLLOW UP

If employees do not meet your expectations, take time to communicate it to them, or the behaviors will not change. If the behaviors do not change, there must be consequences to their actions. No consequence will result in no improvement.

Document negative behaviors that lead to poor results. To effectively terminate an employee and alleviate court hearings, it is necessary to document the performance issues and retain this documentation for future reference. You might need it in the future to support your case. If the employee takes the final straw, never retaliate or hold a grudge, since there is a high risk of this backfiring on the manager. Do not place yourself at risk.

The key is to remain focused on the behaviors, <u>NOT</u> the personality.

TRAIN – MOTIVATE – DELEGATE – FOLLOW UP

MUTUAL RESPECT

IF RESPECT IS GIVEN . . . IT IS TO BE EARNED!

In most cases, if respect is not earned, it is not given in return. You can demand respect, although it is not genuine unless it is earned by you. Remember, you are the leader who should begin the process. If you are respectful to your employees, most of them will respect you in return. Although this is not always the case, it will work the majority of the time. The term is "majority"—keep in mind that *you cannot please all of the people all the time.* You are doing well if you can please most of the people most of the time. Be honest with your staff, as this too will build mutual respect. Do not attempt to bluff them, as you will find that most employees are too smart to be bluffed.

Use the "2-C" method by being courteous and considerate. Do not be vindictive or rude, and do not retaliate. If you practice these negative behaviors, get rid of them NOW, or you will not be treated with the respect you deserve. You must treat all employees equally and fairly, handle yourself in a professional manner, and be a role model. Ask yourself if you practice these qualities consistently. Communicate openly and honestly, as integrity plays a large part in building mutual respect. You must remain calm in your interactions with others.

Do not hold grudges . . . Forgive and forget . . . Move on!

TRAIN – MOTIVATE – DELEGATE – FOLLOW UP

Building mutual respect takes time, effort, and does not happen overnight. It might take weeks or even months, depending on an employee's prior experiences. If trust has been shattered in the past, it can take longer.

Joking could be considered offensive to some employees and not to others, so walk a fine line. Get to know your employees well and be sensitive to what might offend them. What is funny to one person might not be to another.

Benefits of achieving mutual respect:

* Increased cooperation in the workplace.
* Improvement in productivity levels.
* Employees might do you a favor without a second thought.
* Employees might give an "extra effort" on occasion.
* Meeting your budgets and goals becomes much easier.

Results from a lack of mutual respect:

* Poor attitudes.
* Low employee morale.
* Poor customer service.
* Lack of teamwork.
* Productivity goals are harder to meet.

TRAIN – MOTIVATE – DELEGATE – FOLLOW UP

5
STEPS OF SUCCESS

(S.O.S.)

Discussions between a supervisor and an employee must be corrective in nature rather than punitive. The punitive approach could work against the company if the employee turns "sour." If they go sour, they will generally search for the "loopholes" to *not* perform their duties effectively, and still appear to be productive.

STEP I - <u>Supervisor:</u> Identify the specific performance deficiency. Discuss the cause and result of the deficiency.

STEP II - <u>Employee:</u> Acknowledge the performance deficiency and understand the supervisor's concerns.

STEP III - <u>Supervisor:</u> Ask the employee for their feedback on how to correct the deficiency.

STEP IV - <u>Supervisor and Employee:</u> Get a mutual agreement to correct the deficiency.

STEP V - <u>Supervisor:</u> Thank the employee for their commitment to correct the work practices.

Always take notes during an employee/supervisor discussion and retain them for future reference.

TRAIN – MOTIVATE – DELEGATE – FOLLOW UP

SUPPORTING CHANGE
In The Workplace

Change is absolutely necessary to remain competitive in the ever-changing business world. Although some change does not happen for the better, most does. Products change along with customer demand, values change, the cost of production changes, which causes businesses to change. Some people will resist change, although it is usually a move in the right direction, and others will adapt well. Change in the workplace requires support, and feedback is necessary to fine-tune the changes as they evolve, or they could be at risk of failing. How do you know that new ideas, inventions, and updates won't be better if you do not try them? *You don't!* How do you think the microwave and the computer came to exist? What about the VCR, DVD, cell phones, and the newest electronic gizmos that are currently in the works? It is all about "change."

As a manager, you are the leader of change in your organization. If you do not bring about positive changes, no one will. Do not be leery of trying new ideas to achieve greater results. The sky is the limit! Some of your best ideas could come from the employees that work for you. Do not be reluctant to toss out change that has not shown results, as long as you have allowed a reasonable time for implementation.

At some point change will be necessary if your company is to remain profitable, so why not accept it as a way of life? If you expect change to occur, it will not be such a shock when it does happen. Change also breaks the boring routine that seasoned employees can fall into. Change is necessary for the organization to stay in business after your retirement, so everyone will be able to draw from the fund in their later years.

Be flexible to understand and adapt to changing environments, which will expand your career options as well as lead to greater company success. Why is it necessary to support change in the workplace?

1) You will not get others to "buy in" if you do not support it yourself.
2) The workplace will not improve if you are resistant to trying new ideas and approaches.
3) If you explain the reasons for the change prior, employees will be more understanding and cooperative.
4) Over 50 percent of the workforce could be resistant to change.
5) People become accustomed to a routine that they do not like to deviate from.
6) The work environment will never be perfect. Changes could bring positive improvements.
7) Change can be temporarily disruptive until the dust settles, so patience is important.
8) You are the leader, and you set the tone at work.
9) Negative attitudes breed more negativity, so why should you, as their leader, be negative? *STAY POSITIVE!*

TRAIN – MOTIVATE – DELEGATE – FOLLOW UP

MANAGING CHANGE

In The Workplace

Change generally proves to be a benefit in the long term. There are two types of change: immediate or phase-in over a period of time.

Change must be triggered by you, as the manager, since it will not happen on its own. Waiting for change to happen on its own is similar to waiting to get a winning lottery ticket or becoming a millionaire overnight in Las Vegas, and you know what those chances are!

The urgency of change will depend upon the current situation, and the future impact that the changes will create. Not all change should be implemented within the same timeframe. Is the current situation dragging down sales, ruining employee relationships, or lowering morale in the workplace? All of these are major factors for achieving success or failure. Is the current situation a minor problem that is not affecting the bottom line, such as a need for improved lighting or a bulletin board? *Always* research the cost factor involved and the potential return on your investment.

Take time to communicate changes to your employees that will be directly affected. This will help them to understand the reasons why. As a result, your employees will be more apt to accept and cooperate with the changes. If you do not take the time to explain, you will run a high risk of resistance and/or failure. The time spent *will* be worth the gain.

Changes might not be as successful unless you get the entire team behind you. You *must support* all change whether you agree or disagree with it. No one said you had to like it, as long as you, the manager, show support for it. A leader cannot create change without their followers. Do not leave your followers behind or they might get lost and stray away.

Accomplishing change is simpler than you realize, especially when you have built a team and do it as a group. The more people involved in the creation and the implementation process, the sooner it progresses. Set up a realistic timeline for the implementation, and ask for feedback on a regular basis. This will show that you care how it affects your team, positively or negatively. You will never be absolutely sure of the potential results until you have put the changes in place.

TRAIN – MOTIVATE – DELEGATE – FOLLOW UP

As a manager,

you are only as good
as the employees
working for you!

GOALS
AND
EXPECTATIONS

Chapter
4

TOPICS

Chapter 4
Goals and Expectations

* Goals, Expectations, Limits

* Achieving Your Personal Goals

* Communication Is the Key

* Feedback from Employees

GOALS, EXPECTATIONS, LIMITS

Goals: A goal is similar to a dream. It is defined as a level of achievement that you are striving to attain. In an organization it is necessary to set goals for sales, growth, and profit. It is no secret that goals roll "down hill" from the CEO to the newly hired employee. Everyone must clearly understand the common goals if they are to be met. If goals are not reasonable or attainable, most employees will not take an interest in achieving them, and then the company goals will be a joke to the employees.

Expectations: An expectation is not necessarily a goal. It should be set daily for each employee based upon their knowledge, skill, ability, and level of experience. Too often managers set the same expectations for everyone. Expectations vary depending upon deadlines that arise. The manager must set the expectations and the employees should be striving to meet them. The expectations could be a sales quota, productivity factors (pieces per hour), or they could be completion deadlines.

Limits: A limit is a boundary which is established for the employee. Managers set limits for conduct, lunches, breaks, and unacceptable behavior. Employees must be well informed of their limits; do not assume they know what they are. Policies should always be clear, concise, visible, and easy to read.

ACHIEVING YOUR PERSONAL GOALS

It is not rocket science to understand that you cannot achieve a goal that has not been set! So . . . who determines the goals, and what they are? *YOU DO!* Goals come in all shapes and sizes. You will have relationship goals (marriage), financial goals (retirement account), monetary goals (BMW), and goals in the workplace. The goals at work are somewhat different, since they may or may not give you personal satisfaction. A manager will get personal satisfaction, an employee might not, and this is not uncommon for employees. You cannot expect all employees to gain satisfaction from the job. The employee who is looking for added responsibility or advancement more than likely will. Some people are just working to support their family, have job security, and get a consistent paycheck, and that is perfectly fine. Others want more, such as the next level of salary or promotion. That is where you come in, to develop them and help them to achieve their goal. You should always search for employees who are interested in advancement. Part of your assignment is to recruit and train your replacement for when you are promoted.

As a result of achieving the common goals, everyone becomes a success. The company remains stable and generates profit so everyone continues to get their paycheck. Employees feel good about their job and what they have accomplished as a team. Positive results build confidence in employees, the management staff, and the investors on Wall Street.

COMMUNICATION IS THE KEY

You must take time to effectively communicate the message to your employees. I don't believe communication can ever be sufficient enough! The better your communication skills are, the fewer misunderstandings there will be. Do not become sidetracked with interruptions, pagers, phone calls, etc. There are also times when privacy might be necessary for you, the employee, or both. Based upon the circumstances, ask the employee if they prefer to be in private. It will show respect and that you care about their feelings. Take notes when an important conversation takes place, and be sure to inform them of the note-taking in advance. This is an excellent practice, especially when you are discussing performance issues. If it is in private, close the door and allow them space to breathe so they will be comfortable in your presence. Sense their body language and determine if they appear anxious to get something off their chest. This can be helpful in deciding who should begin. Always be courteous, respectful, and show a sincere interest in them. If the topic is important to the employee, it must be equally important to their manager. If you do not have an immediate response to their concerns, inform them when you will get back to them. *Live up to your word!*

Sense their body language to determine if they want to get something off their chest immediately.

FEEDBACK FROM EMPLOYEES

Two-Way Communication

Employees in various organizations have frequently stated that their opinions do not count. Most decisions that impact the workers are made by higher-level managers that are not actually performing the work. Many times, in large companies especially, employees are not asked for their input. This philosophy is beyond me! An employee's opinion or suggestion could be the best one you receive. Listen to your employees and encourage feedback. They could be your best hidden resource.

Be a great listener who is patient and takes an interest in what employees have to say. They want to know that their opinions count. Do not allow yourself to be distracted or interrupted, which could signal to them that you are not really listening or interested in what they have to say. Take notes of their comments, which will show them that you care. Hold your own comments, until they are finished speaking, allowing them the time needed.

It is to your benefit to encourage feedback from your employees. They just might be holding the key to unlocking the best approach to increasing sales or reducing expenses in your company. Value all your people and the opinions they bring along. They can be a wonderful resource if you make the time for them. It is like undiscovered gold in the mine—you will never know it is there until you start digging. How much you will find depends on how much time you spend digging. The deeper the dig, the more you might find!

Two-way communication must be exactly that. Do not allow communication to be one-sided or you could be heading for a train wreck, and might need to be towed back to a more successful management style! Get your employees involved and ask for their input. Do not be reluctant to share ideas with co-workers and other managers, since we all learn from each other. A good idea could be molded (by others) into an outstanding idea. It is similar to molding clay on a potter's wheel. This is where the process is perfected before it is glazed and sold. The same approach applies to ideas in the workplace.

At the end of a conversation, you have an opportunity to comment, and this is the time to provide feedback. To remain credible with the person, you must get back to them with a response. A lack of credibility will result in the breakdown of two-way communication in the future. You, as the manager, cannot afford to let this happen.

Just like two-way communication is critical in a marriage, it is just as critical in the workplace to achieve long-lasting results!

The best idea you get could come from one of your employees.

Goals and Expectations / Chapter 4

Perfection is an unrealistic expectation

Recognize and reward *progress* in a timely manner

ACHIEVING RESULTS

Chapter
5

TOPICS

Chapter 5
Achieving Results

* Progress Versus Perfection

* Rewards and Recognition

* What Occurs When We Don't Correct Poor Performance

* Achieving Long-Term Results

PROGRESS
VERSUS
PERFECTION

When evaluating an employee's performance, it is extremely important to recognize *PROGRESS*. When issuing recognition you should be rewarding the progress toward meeting the goals. Do not be unreasonable in the expectations you set, and do be on the lookout for individual contributions. Do not expect improvement overnight or you will be at risk of disappointment. Significant progress can take time, and continually recognizing *PROGRESS* will eventually achieve the desired result. Progress can be your child's grade rising from a "D" to a "C," coming closer to the final goal, or simply a move in the right direction. Are you recognizing and rewarding progress, or are you waiting for greater results? Act as though you are looking through a magnifying glass to observe *PROGRESS*.

If you wait until perfection is achieved, you will miss the opportunity to give your employees the recognition necessary to be motivated. Each employee moves and improves at a different pace, therefore it would be unfair to expect the same degree of progress from everyone. When dealing with an individual, you must ask yourself, "What is realistic in terms of progress for this person?" and then communicate that expectation to your employee. Your ability to communicate is the lifeline between you and the people you supervise. If you accept only perfection from your employees, they will sense this, and perhaps give up trying to do their best.

The term "the best" can be misinterpreted. Doing "the best" does not mean achieving perfection. Perfection is an unrealistic expectation that will *not* be achieved. "The best" is considered the most attractive, the wealthiest, the most successful, and so forth. Your goal is to be *the best* manager you can be, so that your company will be the best it can be.

RECOGNIZE

PROGRESS

Look through a magnifying glass to see PROG-RESS!

REWARDS AND RECOGNITION

Progress: Defined as "moving forward or onward." Progress must be recognized and rewarded.

Perfection: Defined as "the quality or condition of being perfect." Never wait until perfection is achieved to begin giving rewards!

Sincerity: Defined as "honesty of mind or intention." A reward means nothing unless you are sincere when you give it!

Thanks: Defined as "I thank you." Ask yourself . . . is a verbal thank you sufficient?

Recognize: Defined as "to acknowledge the existence." Are you spending time to recognize employees?

Appreciate: Defined as "to be conscious of the significance." Are you appreciating the work your employees do?

Exceptional: Defined as "extraordinary." Exceptional work must be verbally recognized!

Reward: Defined as "something given in return for good." Are you using various types of rewards?

Realistic: Defined as "practical rather than visionary." Are you setting realistic goals for employees?

Fair: Defined as "on good terms, open, frank, honest." Are you being fair when giving recognition?

WHAT OCCURS WHEN
WE DON'T CORRECT
POOR PERFORMANCE?

* Poor morale
* Poor attitudes
* Lack of rewards
* Frustration rises
* Sick calls increase
* Stress levels increase
* Goals are not achieved
* Good workers get abused
* Good performers burn out
* Added pressure from the boss
* More employees take advantage
* Good performers become disgusted
* Employees perform at the minimum
* Company might go out of business soon

As you can see . . .
We MUST correct poor performance.

(It is NOT optional)

ACHIEVING LONG-TERM RESULTS
TO
SUCCESS

Short-term results are simple to achieve, although long-term are not quite as easy. Managers must lead by example and set the expectations of what is acceptable. As a manager you will set the tone as well as the pace. The tone is set by an "attitude," and the pace is set by your own work ethic. Your employees are constantly observing you and evaluating what you do. Most employees will follow your lead, so it is important that you are a positive role model.

Long-term success is achieved by adhering to company policies and procedures. If your style of management is "black and white," always remember there is a "gray" page in the back of the manual. Policies and procedures are designed to be followed, although they must remain a bit flexible. Most procedures should not be deviated from.

Long-term success depends on employee dedication, and respect for the company as well as the management team. When employees are treated fairly and honestly, and their contributions are appreciated, their dedication will rise to new levels. Maximizing of sales and productivity will increase profit and will stabilize the entire organization. As a result, there will be plenty of job security and this will lead to improved attitudes, as employees feel confident that their positions are not subject to elimination. We all know that downsizing makes employees nervous, which can distract them from their primary focus.

Have confidence in your employees so they will continue to remain productive when the management staff
is not present. Long-term success relies on a self-managed concept, which can take time and effort to create. It
also depends on the employees being able to work *with*
the management, not against them. Employees working
against the management will eventually lead to failure.
You cannot afford to NOT have your people working *with*
you.

*Long-term success is dependent upon employee
dedication!*

POINTS TO REMEMBER

Achieving Results / Chapter 5

Spend more time searching for the positive.

It will motivate employees and bring positive results.

Closing Comments

In closing . . .

During the twenty-plus years of my management career, I have worked with over thirty different mid-level managers and countless employees. Some managers taught me what approaches worked and others taught what did not work. I learned styles and approaches from everyone I worked for. To be the BEST manager you can be, keep the following points in mind . . .

EFFECTIVE leaders teach:

* Treat employees as mature adults.
* Have confidence in your employees.
* Encourage your employees.
* Recognize and reward employees.
* Communication is critical.
* Be a professional leader.

INEFFECTIVE leaders teach:

* Establishing unrealistic goals is not an incentive.
* Being dishonest deteriorates respect.
* Focusing on the negative brings poor results.
* Lack of mutual respect de-motivates employees.

Always remember: It is not what you have read, it is how you apply the new strategies you learned from reading this book.

---

*I would like to thank my wife, daughter, and son for their patience
while I have been writing this book.
Their support has been appreciated!*

GLOSSARY

Accountability—A follow up process to ensure completeness

Autocratic Manager—Bold, direct, and demanding approach

Behaviors—Actions, not personality traits

Empower— Encouraging employees to be self-managed

Human Relation Skills—Utilizing effective "people skills"

Intimidator—One who demands or threatens to get results

Micro-Manager—One who will shadow their employees

Maintenance Manager—Maintaining the status quo

Managing—Overseeing, directing and following up

Morale—How employees feel about their job

Slug—An employee who works at an extremely slow pace

S.O.S.—A term in this book to describe the "Steps of Success"

Superstar—An employee who excels beyond the requirements

Team—Two or more people working toward a common goal

Index

H

I

L

M

P

R

By referring this book to family, friends, or associate managers (your boss), you are eligible for a one-dollar rebate on the purchase price of this book. Fill out the attached coupon (below) with the name and address of your referral and mail it to the following address:

Management S.O.S.
P. O. Box #2434
Elk Grove, CA
95759-2434

Include: Original purchase receipt (no copies accepted) along with a self-addressed stamped envelope for the rebate, to be returned to you within 6 to 8 weeks. Feel free to submit your comments regarding this book along with the enclosed coupon. This information we receive will be used strictly for advertising this book to your referral of choice. Personal information or the referral names will NOT be transferred or sold to anyone. OUR PROMISE!

Cut Here--Cut Here

REBATE REFERRAL
$1 Referral Value

Name of Referral

Address

City, State, Zip

Original Book Purchase Receipt MUST Be Included
For Your Rebate

If you appreciated and gained knowledge from this book, be ready for the next book in the series of . . .

MANAGEMENT STEPS OF SUCCESS S.O.S

Improving
Performance

Author
George W. Kaminsky

About the Author

The task of managing employees is a never-ending challenge. I've managed a countless number of employees during my career, ranging from entry-level to mid-level management positions. My experience includes retail manager, district manager and field training coordinator, as well as supervisor for a governmental agency which included a unionized workforce. It was my job to figure out what motivated each employee, as well as to understand their habits and work ethic. To increase my knowledge, I took various courses in business, management, and human relation skills.

I joined the management team, not primarily for the extra money, but to make a difference in the organization. I saw the way employees were being treated and thought there was a great deal of room for improvement, so I decided to take the next step... and climb the ladder. It was my goal to create a positive change in the company, and I worked hard at treating employees the same way that I wanted to be treated. I focused on rewarding employees who performed well, and worked with others to improve negative attitudes, as well as unsatisfactory performance. I built a "team" of employees who took pride in their work and had positive attitudes. I would like to share the knowledge I've gained through my personal experiences, with you. Remember... As a manager, you are only as good as the people who work for you!